Secrets of the Journey

LEADERSHIP SECRETS

FOR

EXCELLENCE & INCREASE

5

MIKE MURDOCK

SECRETS OF THE JOURNEY, VOLUME 5
ISBN 1-56394-063-9
Copyright © 1997 by Mike Murdock
First Printing 40,000 Copies

Published by Wisdom International
P. O. Box 99 • Dallas, Texas 75221

Unless otherwise indicated, all Scripture quotations are taken from the *King James Version* of the Bible.

TABLE OF CONTENTS

≈ Philippians 4:13 ≈

"I can do all things through
Christ which strengtheneth me."

❧ 1 ❧

BECOME AN ENEMY TO YOUR WEAKNESS.

You cannot play with a Weakness in your life.

I have been in the ministry for 31 years and watched incredible, powerful and extraordinary men fall from their thrones into ashes. Good men. Articulate men. Brilliant men. But, a *tiny Weakness*, like a small cancer, began to eat its way into their lives. Greed, lust, lying, prayerlessness, gossip grew until that Weakness became a raging inferno. The small puppy became a rabid monster.

Your Weakness may presently be at the embryonic state. Perhaps the size of an acorn. Nobody else can see it yet. You may even joke about it. But you cannot afford to play with a Weakness in your life.

You see, when you are not victorious, you will become miserable. That misery creates agitation. That agitation will cause you to lash out at those you love, thus destroying the very foundation of your life.

Here are 40 facts about your Weakness:

1. *The war of your life is between your Strength and your Weakness.* (Read Galatians 5:17.)

2. *Everyone has a Weakness.* "All have sinned." (See Romans 3:23.)

3. *Your Weakness will bond you with the wrong people.* Remember Samson and Delilah. (Judges 16:4-20.)

4. *Your Weakness can multiply.* A little leaven always leaveneth the whole lump. (See 1 Corinthians 5:6-8.)

5. Your *Weakness should be confronted when it first emerges at it's early sign of exposure.*

6. *Your Weakness separates you from the right people.* Adam withdrew from God in the Garden after he sinned. (See Genesis 3:8.)

7. *Few will confront their Weakness with the proper weaponry, the Word of God.* "Wherewithal shall a young man cleanse his ways? by taking heed thereto according to thy word," (Psalm 119:9).

8. *Your Weakness can emerge at any time in your life, including your closing years.* "Cast me not off in the time of old age; forsake me not when my strength faileth" (Psalm 71:9).

9. *Your Weakness is the entry point for Satan and demonic spirits.* Satan *entered* Judas. See John 13:26.

10. *Your Weakness cannot be overcome with humanism, human philosophy, explanations, and self will power.* If your Weakness could be overcome by yourself, the blood of Jesus is powerless and the Holy Spirit is unnecessary. "Ye shall receive power, after that the Holy Ghost is come upon you," (Acts 1:8).

11. *Satan will invest whatever time is necessary to nurture a small Weakness into a raging wolf that destroys you.* Keep resisting. (Matthew 4:3-10.)

12. *Your Weakness does not necessarily have to be confessed to everybody.* But you must admit it to

yourself and to your heavenly Father. (See Psalm 34:18 and James 5:16.)

13. *Your heavenly Father is fully aware of your Weakness.* (It matters to Him. He reaches out to you to annihilate it.) "He remembered that they were but flesh" (Psalm 78:39). (See also Psalm 103:14.)

14. *Somebody is assigned by hell to fuel and strengthen your Weakness.* Delilah was sent by Satan to destroy Samson. (Judges 16:4-5.)

15. *The lives and futures of those you love are awaiting your overcoming and triumph over your Weakness.* Your victory means victory for them! When David killed Goliath the entire nation of Israel changed seasons. Your family is sitting in fear of their own weaknesses that can destroy them. But they will be strengthened when they see *you* victorious over your Weakness.

16. *Your Weakness searches for every opportunity to grow.* (Read Matthew 6:22-23.)

17. *Your Weakness will embrace and seize any friendship that permits it, allows it to exist and finds it tolerable.*

18. *What others may not consider a Weakness, God knows is your Weakness.* Your conscience confirms it, too.

19. Every Weakness *grows.* It cannot stay the same. It is being fed and nourished or destroyed and starved. "A little leaven leaveneth the whole lump" (1 Corinthians 5:6).

20. *You must starve your Weakness a day at a time.* Make no room for the flesh. (Romans 13:14.)

21. *Your Weakness will not remain in you alone but will move toward others, and infect those around*

you. It will become bigger and *bigger,* stronger and *stronger.* It considers you, your dreams, and future to be its greatest Enemy.

22. *Your Weakness hates your Strengths.* You see, your Strengths are a threat to your Weakness.

23. *Your Weakness does not want to stay small.*

24. *Your Weakness does not want to remain insignificant.* It craves expression.

25. *Your Weakness will become angry when it is ignored.*

26. *Your Weakness has a will of its own.* "I find then a law, that, when I would do good, evil is present with me," (Romans 7:21).

27. *Your Weakness has an agenda, a plan to take over your life and sabotage it.* "When lust hath conceived, it bringeth forth sin: and sin, when it is finished, bringeth forth death," (James 1:15).

28. *Your Weakness despises the exploits and accomplishments of your Strength.* (Judges 16:6.)

29. *Your Weakness must be destroyed, not tolerated and enjoyed occasionally.* (See 1 Samuel 15:7-10.)

30. *God will permit you to enjoy many victories.* Even while your Weakness is *in its beginning stages.* He is long-suffering and merciful. He gives you chance after chance, opportunity after opportunity to repent and reach for deliverance. Jesus cried, "...how often would I have gathered thy children together, even as a hen gathereth her chickens under her wings, and ye would not!" (Matthew 23:37b).

31. *When you justify your Weakness, it laughs with glee knowing that in due time, it will displace a Strength in your life.*

32. *Your Weakness can only be overcome by the*

Word of God in your life when you confront it. Satan attempts to camouflage your Weakness, wrapping it in acceptable vocabulary. "Ye shall be as gods..." (Genesis 3:5.) Jesus used the Word as a weapon. (Matthew 4:1-11.)

33. *God wants to grow your Strength and destroy your Weakness.* "Reckon ye also yourselves to be dead indeed unto sin, but alive unto God through Jesus Christ our Lord" (Romans 6:11).

34. *Your Weakness has cousins.* It will not rest until everyone of them come to visit and take up a void in your life. The adultery of David *birthed* the murder of Uriah. (2 Samuel 11:1-17.)

35. *Nobody has merely one Weakness.* Your strongest Weakness invites another one to come and visit.

36. *Your victory over your Weakness will unlock victories for others.* Even if they are unaware of your Weakness.

37. *Your Weakness is always an enemy to Thankfulness.* You see, you are never thankful for a Weakness. Weakness is unappreciated. It reacts vehemently and begins a relentless journey to choke out any sign of Thankfulness. It knows you hate it. It never receives the praise, adoration and recognition that your Strength receives.

38. *God makes every effort to reveal your Weakness to you before it destroys you.* "And the Lord said, Simon, Simon, behold, Satan hath desired to have you, that he may sift you as wheat," (Luke 22:31).

39. *It's possible to know and recognize your own Weakness before others know it.* Peter discovered this. (Matthew 26:33-35; 73-75.)

40. *Overcoming your Weakness brings incredible rewards for all eternity.* (Revelation 3.)

Your Weakness is not a whimpering puppy to be fed when hungry. Your Weakness is a deadly, rabid wolf to be despised, rejected and destroyed.

Don't make friends with your Weakness. Don't bond with it. Become an enemy to your Weakness. Make Weakness your enemy.

It is One of the Secrets of the Journey.

❦ 2 ❦

ALWAYS ALLOW OTHERS ROOM TO TURN AROUND.

—————➤•◦•◀—————

Everybody makes mistakes.
Everybody deserves the chance to change.
Allow them to do so.

When pressure increases, those around you are affected and influenced. Their stress can affect you. The constant demands of others often birth impatience and mistakes. During these moments, *your mercy is necessary.*

Wrong words are often blurted out.
Inaccurate assessments are made.
Wrong decisions are made.

Think back upon your own life. Many frustrations drove you to that moment of indiscretion, those cutting words and angry outbursts.

Allow forgiveness.

Don't force others to live by their past bad decisions. Whatever you sow will come back to you a hundred times. So give them space to come back into the relationship *with dignity.* Jesus taught it. "Blessed are the merciful: for they shall obtain mercy" (Matthew 5:7).

Forgive them 490 times. "Then came Peter to him,

and said, Lord, how oft shall my brother sin against me, and I forgive him? till seven times? Jesus saith unto him, I say not unto thee, Until seven times: but, Until seventy times seven" (Matthew 18:21-22).

Forgive seventy times seven. Give them *enough* time. Things are happening you cannot see. Sometimes it takes weeks and even months for some to realize and admit their mistakes.

Give them a season of *solitude.*

Give them opportunities for *expression*, an opportunity to explain themselves. They may *not* know the right choice of words the *first time.* Be willing to *listen longer*.

Give them time to evaluate *every* part of the puzzle. You may be looking at one part. They are considering many different factors they have yet to discuss with you.

Give them time to discover the truth *about you.* You already know yourself. They do not. They do not know all of your *flaws.* They do not know all of your *capabilities.* They do not understand your *memories.* Your pain. Your goals or dreams.

They may be looking at now.

You are looking at tomorrow.

Allow others space to correct their mistakes.

It's One of the Secrets of the Journey.

≈ 3 ≈

SECURE A RECEIPT FOR EVERYTHING.

Document every purchase.

Develop the habit of keeping receipts on everything you buy. When I leave the airport, I secure a receipt for the fifty cents it costs. Not because I need the reimbursement, but I need the *habit* of asking for a receipt to be emphasized and kept permanent in my life.

I want the habit to become *instinctive*, not requiring my memory or attention.

Here Are Six Benefits In Keeping Receipts:

1. *The habit of keeping receipts will help you with your taxes.* When you complete your income tax forms at the end of the year, you'll be thankful for every receipt that can be deducted from your Income Tax Return.

2. *Keeping receipts keeps you reminded of where your money has been spent.* This is important. Expenses are usually much more than what you had originally planned for. It will help you in budgeting and planning ahead.

3. *When you keep receipts, you send a message of organization and order.* You know what you are talking about and it shows.

4. *When you keep receipts, you increase the*

confidence of others toward you. They will consider your opinion valuable on other matters as well.

5. *When an employee approaches his boss for a reimbursement without a receipt, this sends a damaged message to him.* Were they sloppy in organizing their receipts? Did they really *secure* a receipt? Did they actually spend the money? Do they not care about the finances of the business?

When you fail to keep receipts:

a. You portray sloppiness and disorder.
b. You cause others to *doubt* everything you say.
c. You *slow down* the reimbursement process.
d. You create a climate of *suspicion.*
e. You send a message of rebellion and stubbornness.

6. *Keeping receipts can help protect your reputation for integrity.*

Something interesting happened many years ago. When I left a motel in Kentucky, I pulled out my credit card to pay for my personal telephone calls. (The host church always pays for the room and food. But, I always pay for the telephone calls, faxes or other items.) I was in a hurry to the airport. I placed the receipt in my little leather bag.

In those days, I would often minister several weeks of meetings before returning home. Receipts always piled up. After a few weeks, I always have a stack of receipts that I cannot begin to explain to anyone! Especially when I'm taking flights, shoving $5.00 bills in the hands of bellmen at the motel or the hands of a skycap at the airport. When I am busy making change and running through airports, receipts often become a blur. (Since then, I try to *write the description of the purchase on every receipt.* This triggers my memory two or three weeks later when reviewing it with my bookkeeper.)

Thirty days later, the telephone rang. I was in my little garage working at my desk. (It was my office at the time in Houston, Texas.) It was my pastor friend from Kentucky. He sounded distant and rather cool. He plunged in without the normal pleasantries.

"Hello, Mike? I just wanted to know why you did not pay your own telephone calls here at the motel when you checked out?"

He did not even bother asking me if I had paid the hotel for the telephone bill or not. He addressed me fully confident that the motel staff had given him accurate information.

I was taken aback. In fact, I felt rather agitated that he had not sought an explanation from me *first.* (The telephone bill was not that high, anyhow.) But, I explained to him that I *had* paid my own telephone bill.

"Well, they have just charged the church for it again, if you did pay it." He actually sounded like he believed the hotel over *me!*

I asked him to hold the line for a few moments. I began to dig through my desk drawer. Miraculously, I found the receipt in a stack of receipts in my desk drawer. I pulled it and gave the details to him on the phone. Then, I made a copy and mailed it to him. (This was before the creation of fax machines! May God bless the man or woman who created the fax machine!) The point is, my receipt salvaged my reputation.

The answer is simple. *Always get a receipt.*

Solomon was meticulous about record keeping. Every single animal used in a meal in the palace was accounted for. "Be thou diligent to know the state of thy flocks, and look well to thy herds" (Proverbs 27:23). Why? "For riches are not for ever" (Proverbs 27:24a).

Successful people secure *receipts* for everything. *It's One of the Secrets of the Journey.*

∼ 4 ∼

Never Assume That Your Instructions Have Been Followed.

Confirm everything.

I have marveled how so many have kept their jobs over the years. Few seem to *follow-through* on instructions given to them by their supervisors.

True, there are a few close to you who may have proven themselves over a long period of time. They understand you. They are diligent, aggressive and trustworthy. But my own experience is that there are *less than five people* in your life that you can count on to *fully complete an assigned task with excellence.*

Four Ways To Recognize An Undependable Person:

1. *They do not keep paper and pen in their hand.* Never trust an employee who does not regularly carry paper and pen in their hand to follow through on something you've asked them to do. *Never.*

2. *They make no attempt to ever reach for paper and pen to document the instruction.* They simply nod. They do not *write* it down. They do not *document* it. They trust their memory. Bank on it — the instruction will be *forgotten* in their busyness.

3. *They ask no additional questions about the assignment or instruction.* Few instructions are complete at the beginning. They *should* be asking:

    a. Is there a *deadline* on this?

    b. When do you need a *report back* on the results of this telephone call?

    c. Is there anything *additional* I should know about?

When additional questions are never asked, following an instruction given, *they're not giving any thought to it.*

4. They always reply, "I will *try* to get to that, sir." *Believe me, they won't get to it.* The very word "*try*" gives them away.

Seven Things You Should Remember When You Give Instructions To Others.

1. Communicate clearly *the importance* of the instruction.

2. Give the instruction to *one person* only.

3. *Document the date* you gave the instruction.

4. Require a continuous *progress report.*

5. *Agree* upon the expected deadline for the completion of the task.

6. Never give an instruction to someone *incompetent to complete it.*

7. Never *assume* your instructions have been completed. Follow through.

It's One of the Secrets of the Journey.

∾ 5 ∾

ALWAYS CLOSE DOORS GENTLY.

Relationships do not always last forever.

So, it is important to *exit* every Door of Friendship properly. You cannot enter the next season of your life with joy unless you exit your present season *correctly*.

Jesus finished His work on earth. He cried out from the cross, "It is finished!" Salvation was complete. Redemption had taken place. He had paid the price for the sins of man. Three days later, the resurrection would take place. He would return to the Father where He would make intercession for you and me. He finished *properly* — with the approval of the Father.

Solomon finished the temple. It was an incredible feat. Some value his temple today at over $500 billion dollars. He was respected, pursued and celebrated. He *completed* what he started.

Paul finished his race. He fought a good fight, kept his course and finished the race. He was a success in the eyes of God. He made his exit from his earthly ministry with grace, passion and dignity.

Your life is a collection of *Beginnings.*

It is also a collection of *Exits*.

You will not stay in your present job forever. You will someday leave your present position. Your supervisor today could be another acquaintance in your life next year. Close the relationship with dignity.

Eight Keys To Remember When A Relationship Is Ending.

1. *Close every Door gently.* Do not slam Doors. Do not kick Doors. Do not yell at Doors. They are Doors *through which you may need to return again* in the future. The attitude of *your exit* determines if you can ever walk back through that Door again. "A soft answer turneth away wrath: but grevious words stir up anger," (Proverbs 15:1).

2. *Close Doors with forgiveness.* Unforgiveness is poisonous. It is the cancer that will destroy you from within. Release others to God. Permit Him to do the penalizing or correcting. Like Joseph, recognize that the ultimate plan of God will bring your promotion. (See Romans 8:28.)

3. *Close the Doors with kindness.* If your fianceé leaves you with cutting and bitter words, thank the Holy Spirit for salvaging you. Perhaps she was not your *Proverbs 31 Woman* after all. "...in her tongue is the law of kindness" (Proverbs 31:26b).

4. *Close every Door with promises fulfilled.* Don't leave your job until you have finished *what you promised.* Complete every vow. *Whatever* the cost. Integrity is easy to test. Simply ask yourself: Did I fulfill my promise? (See Ecclesiastes 5:4,5.)

When people lose you in the Forest of Words, apply this Principle of Vow Fulfillment. Forget the blaming, complaining and accusations. This principle reveals everything you need to know about another.

5. *Close every Door with integrity.* Few will do it. *People are rarely angry for the reason they tell you.* Employees rarely leave for the reason they explain. Much is never discussed. The trap of deception is deadly. It begins when you deceive *yourself*, then, those around you. Always be honest to others about *the reason* for the Doors closing. It is not necessary to give *every* detail. But it is important that the details you give are *accurate*.

6. *Close every Door with courage.* It is not always easy to close a Door that the Holy Spirit requires. So, closing that Door requires uncommon courage to face the future without that person. Remember the precious Holy Spirit will never leave you nor forsake you. (See John 14:16.) He opens Doors. He closes Doors. He is the Bridge to every person in your future.

7. *Close every Door with expectation of promotion.* "For promotion cometh neither from the east, nor from the west, nor from the south. But God is the judge: he putteth down one, and setteth up another," (Psalms 75:6-7).

8. *Close every Door by the timing of the Holy Spirit.* Don't close it in a fit of anger. Do not close the Door because of a misunderstanding that erupts. Don't close it just because someone *recommends* that you exit. Know the timing of God. (See Ecclesiastes 3:1-8.)

A young man sat in my kitchen a few weeks ago. I was quite concerned. He wanted a position in my ministry. I asked him about his relationship with his previous boss, my pastor friend. He avoided the issue continually. In fact, I had to ask him the question four or five times before I got a partial answer. At the end of the conversation, he explained his financial dilemma. He had left a job before ever securing another one. I explained to him how foolish this was. If God were moving him, He would tell him the place he was to go.

When God told Elijah to leave the brook, Zarephath was scheduled. (See 1 Kings 17.)

When the Israelites left Egypt, Canaan was their determined destination. (See Exodus 13.)

God always brings you out of a place to bring you into another place. So, close every Door with God's timing. When you close Doors gently, news will travel. Good news.

That's One of the Golden Secrets of the Journey.

≈ 6 ≈

ALWAYS HONOR
THE SCHEDULE
OF OTHERS.

─────≫•◦•≪─────

Respect the responsibilities of another.

I had finished a two-day School of the Holy Spirit up north. It had been a glorious two days. The presence of God was so powerful. I loved being with my friends and partners, as always.

However, due to the airline schedule, I had to leave 30 minutes earlier than planned. Another minister was going to finish the session for me. Because of the airline schedule, two flights were necessary and would let me arrive at my destination approximately at 1:00 a.m. in the morning. My schedule was hectic. In fact, I would barely make the church where I was scheduled. So, I announced to everyone present that my plane schedule was tight. I would be unable to stay afterwards for any additional conversation.

Yet, as I was rushing toward the door with my briefcase, my associate by my side, five to seven people stopped me. Standing in front of me, they insisted that I autograph my books. Some insisted that I hear about an experience they had had.

Each one of them *totally ignored my own*

schedule. They had no concern whatsoever.

Did they love me? Not really. They loved *themselves*. Their only obsession was *to get something* they wanted, regardless of the toll it took on me. My needs meant nothing. My own schedule was unimportant to them.

The Holy Spirit is always offended by such insensitivity and uncaring for others, "...in honour preferring one another;" (Romans 12:10b).

Always make sure your time with someone is appropriate for their schedule. (See Ecclesiastes 3:1-8.)

Reject manipulating, intimidating and abusive words. "You never take time for me" is simply an attempt to intimidate you. Statements like, "You *never* have time for me. You always have time for everyone else!" is *victim* vocabulary. This kind of person has no true regard for others. They are obsessed with themselves. You cannot give them enough time or attention to satisfy them.

Always mark those who show disregard and disrespect for your time, the most precious gift God gave you. If they don't respect your time, neither will they respect your wisdom.

When You Honor the Schedule of Others, Favor Will Flow.

It's One of the Secrets of the Journey.

☙ 7 ☙

Sow During Times Of Crisis.

————▶◆◀————

Crisis creates fear.

It happened to me several years ago. Through a parade of tragedies, personal and ministry, I suddenly faced bankruptcy. I owed much more than what I owned. I did not know what to do. I prayed, fasted and used every business principle I knew. The wall refused to move. It was a mountain of debt that nothing could shake.

I became intimidated. I felt like a failure. Other ministries were flourishing and building huge buildings. I couldn't even pay my CPA $1,500 to secure a financial statement to present to the bank for a loan. (And, though I had known him for years, he refused to do it for me!) I met with successful businessmen who offered to loan me $250,000 — if I would pay them $50,000 immediately. I did not even have $5,000 cash to my name.

During times like these, Satan can really appear overpowering. It's hard to believe that your pain will ever pass.

I couldn't think straight. I would sit numbly in various meetings around tables of negotiation. My mind was in shock. My heart lost its fight. I could not budge the wall of debt. Sometimes, during the battles of life, you will be tempted to withdraw, become timid and passive. You see, Satan is a bully. Bullies delight in shy, timid "peacemakers."

Three Things I've Learned To Do During Crisis.

1. *You must develop a fighting spirit.* It is very important. "Resist the devil, and he will flee from you" (James 4:7b).

2. *You must run toward your Goliath.* David did. But he did not come in his own strength against his enemy. He came "in the name of the LORD."

3. *You must sow during crisis.* Crisis is the place of miracles. It is not the place to shrink back, quit and hoard your sowing. I was so tempted to stop giving. I felt that the ministry needed to "keep the tithe for itself."

Crisis distorts every picture of prosperity.

Why is crisis an important time to sow?

▶ Sowing births *expectation* and hope.

▶ *Expectation is the only magnet that attracts the miracle provision God has promised.*

"Without faith it is impossible to please him: for he that cometh to God must believe that he is, and that he is a rewarder of them that diligently seek him" (Hebrews 11:6).

Refusing to sow will destroy your own ability *to expect* a miracle. A farmer can only expect a harvest *after* he has planted seed. Similarly, your sowing is what births your *expectation.* Your expectation is the current that brings the one hundredfold return Jesus promised.

Nothing is going to change for you financially until you can fuel and energize *expectation* within you.

Crisis actually magnifies the size of your Seed in the eyes of God. Your Seed will increase in its influence with God *because of your crisis.*

Let me explain. Jesus was watching the offering being received one day. (See Mark 12:41-42.)

Later He shared with His disciples. "This poor widow hath cast more in, than all they which have cast into the treasury: For all they did cast in of their abundance; but she of her want did cast in all that she had, even all her living" (Mark 12:43b-44). She was poor, but she attracted the attention of Jesus. Why? Her financial crisis enlarged her Seed in the eyes of God. She gave more than everyone else, in His opinion, *because of her crisis.*

That's why it is important to plant Seed when your back is against the wall and you have very little. Your Seed will carry *more* weight, influence and potential for increase than a much larger Seed will have later when you are doing quite well.

Thousands hoard during a crisis. *It is the most unwise thing you could ever do.* If you will sow during times of famine, your Seed will move the heavens and open the windows. God will pour you out a blessing you can hardly contain.

Sow Your Greatest Seed During Your Greatest Crisis.

It's One of the Secrets of the Journey.

Receive your gift copy when you sow a $58.00 Seed.

DECISION

Will You Accept Jesus As Savior Of Your Life Today?

The Bible says, "That if thou shalt confess with thy mouth the Lord Jesus, and shall believe in thine heart that God hath raised Him from the dead, thou shalt be saved. For with the heart man believeth unto righteousness; and with the mouth confession is made unto salvation."(Rom. 10:9-10)

To receive Jesus Christ as Lord and Savior of your life, please pray this prayer from your heart today!

"Dear Jesus, I believe that you died for me and rose again on the third day. I confess I am a sinner. I need Your love and forgiveness. Come into my life, forgive my sins, and give me eternal life. I confess You now as my Lord. Thank You for my salvation, Your peace and joy. Amen."

FREE!
My Best-Selling Book
"101 Wisdom Keys"

You can receive today your personal gift copy of this life-changing book. Contained inside this volume are some of the most powerful Wisdom Keys God has ever imparted to my heart. Make this book your personal Wisdom Guide. Keep it handy. Apply the principles. Your life will be transformed forever! It is my Seed of Blessing into every friend who pursues the Wisdom of God.

Order Today!
Or Call Toll Free:
1-888-WISDOM-1

VICTORY PAK 1

◆ **The Jesus Book**

"Everything God Ever Said About His Son Jesus." This book answers your many questions about Jesus, His birth, betrayal, miracles; answered by Scripture only.

◆ **Battle Techniques For War-Weary Saints**

◆ **The Sex Trap**

◆ **Ten Lies Many People Believe About Money**

VICTORY PAK 2

◆ **The God Book**

"Everything You Always Wanted To Know About God But Were Afraid To Ask." 127 questions answered by Scripture only.

◆ **The Greatest Success Habit On Earth**

◆ **5 Steps Out Of Depression**

◆ **Four Forces That Guarantee Career Success**

4 Books For Just $10⁰⁰!

Product Order Form - *Please Print Clearly!*

Code	Name of Item	Qty	Price	Total
PAKVP1	Victory Pak Number One		$10.00	
PAKVP2	Victory Pak Number Two		$10.00	

SORRY NO C.O.D.'s *Canada should add 20% to the total cost of items to accommodate currency difference.	(Canada add 20%)	$
	Sub-Total	$
	Add 10% Shipping	$
	My Seed-Faith Gift for Your Ministry	$
	Total Enclosed	$

Name

Address

City

State | Zip | Home Telephone

❑ Cash ❑ Check ❑ Money Order ❑ Visa ❑ MC ❑ AMEX

Card # | Exp. Date

Signature _____

Mail Form To: Mike Murdock•P.O. Box 99•Dallas, TX•75221 Or Call Toll Free: 1-888-WISDOM-1

VP92

ORDER FORM THE MIKE MURDOCK WISDOM LIBRARY
(All books paperback unless indicated otherwise.)

QTY	CODE	BOOK TITLE	USA / £	TOTAL
	B01	WISDOM FOR WINNING	$10 / 7 £	
	B02	5 STEPS OUT OF DEPRESSION	$ 2 / 1 £	
	B03	THE SEX TRAP	$ 2 / 1 £	
	B04	10 LIES PEOPLE BELIEVE ABOUT MONEY	$ 2 / 1 £	
	B05	FINDING YOUR PURPOSE IN LIFE	$ 2 / 1 £	
	B06	CREATING TOMORROW THROUGH SEED-FAITH	$ 2 / 1 £	
	B07	BATTLE TECHNIQUES FOR WAR WEARY SAINTS	$ 2 / 1 £	
	B08	ENJOYING THE WINNING LIFE	$ 2 / 1 £	
	B09	FOUR FORCES/GUARANTEE CAREER SUCCESS	$ 2 / 1 £	
	B10	THE BRIDGE CALLED DIVORCE	$ 2 / 1 £	
	B11	DREAM SEEDS	$ 9 / 6 £	
	B12	YOUNG MINISTERS HANDBOOK	$20 /13£	
	B13	SEEDS OF WISDOM ON DREAMS AND GOALS	$ 3 / 2 £	
	B14	SEEDS OF WISDOM ON RELATIONSHIPS	$ 3 / 2 £	
	B15	SEEDS OF WISDOM ON MIRACLES	$ 3 / 2 £	
	B16	SEEDS OF WISDOM ON SEED-FAITH	$ 3 / 2 £	
	B17	SEEDS OF WISDOM ON OVERCOMING	$ 3 / 2 £	
	B18	SEEDS OF WISDOM ON HABITS	$ 3 / 2 £	
	B19	SEEDS OF WISDOM ON WARFARE	$ 3 / 2 £	
	B20	SEEDS OF WISDOM ON OBEDIENCE	$ 3 / 2 £	
	B21	SEEDS OF WISDOM ON ADVERSITY	$ 3 / 2 £	
	B22	SEEDS OF WISDOM ON PROSPERITY	$ 3 / 2 £	
	B23	SEEDS OF WISDOM ON PRAYER	$ 3 / 2 £	
	B24	SEEDS OF WISDOM ON FAITH TALK	$ 3 / 2 £	
	B25	SEEDS OF WISDOM ONE YEAR DEVOTIONAL	$10 / 7 £	
	B26	THE GOD BOOK	$10 / 7 £	
	B27	THE JESUS BOOK	$10 / 7 £	
	B28	THE BLESSING BIBLE	$10 / 7 £	
	B29	THE SURVIVAL BIBLE	$10 / 7 £	
	B30	TEENAGERS TOPICAL BIBLE	$ 6 / 4 £	
	B30L	TEENAGERS TOPICAL BIBLE (LEATHER)	$20 /13£	
	B31	ONE-MINUTE TOPICAL BIBLE	$12 / 8 £	
	B32	MINISTER'S TOPICAL BIBLE	$ 6 / 4 £	
	B33	BUSINESSMAN'S TOPICAL BIBLE	$ 6 / 4 £	
	B33L	BUSINESSMAN'S TOPICAL BIBLE (LEATHER)	$20 /13£	
	B34L	GRANDPARENT'S TOPICAL BIBLE (LEATHER)	$20 /13£	
	B35	FATHER'S TOPICAL BIBLE	$ 6 / 4 £	
	B35L	FATHER'S TOPICAL BIBLE (LEATHER)	$20 /13£	
	B36	MOTHER'S TOPICAL BIBLE	$ 6 / 4 £	
	B36L	MOTHER'S TOPICAL BIBLE (LEATHER)	$20 /13£	
	B37	NEW CONVERT'S BIBLE	$ 6 / 4 £	
	B38	THE WIDOW'S TOPICAL BIBLE	$ 6 / 4 £	
	B39	THE DOUBLE DIAMOND PRINCIPLE	$ 9 / 6 £	
	B40	WISDOM FOR CRISIS TIMES	$ 9 / 6 £	
	B41	THE GIFT OF WISDOM (VOLUME ONE)	$ 8 / 5 £	
	B42	ONE-MINUTE BUSINESSMAN'S DEVOTIONAL	$10 / 7 £	
	B43	ONE-MINUTE BUSINESSWOMAN'S DEVOTIONAL	$10 / 7 £	
	B44	31 SECRETS FOR CAREER SUCCESS	$10 / 7 £	
	B45	101 WISDOM KEYS	$ 7 / 4 £	
	B46	31 FACTS ABOUT WISDOM	$ 7 / 4 £	
	B47	THE COVENANT OF 58 BLESSINGS	$ 8 / 5 £	
	B48	31 KEYS TO A NEW BEGINNING	$ 7 / 4 £	
	B49	31 SECRETS OF THE PROVERBS 31 WOMAN	$ 7 / 4 £	
	B50	ONE-MINUTE POCKET BIBLE FOR ACHIEVERS	$ 5 / 3 £	
	B51	ONE-MINUTE POCKET BIBLE FOR FATHERS	$ 5 / 3 £	
	B52	ONE-MINUTE POCKET BIBLE FOR MOTHERS	$ 5 / 3 £	

MAIL TO: DR. MIKE MURDOCK •THE WISDOM TRAINING CENTER • P.O. BOX 99 • DALLAS, TX 75221
(940) 464-3020 OR USA CALL TOLL FREE 1-888-WISDOM-1

Qty	Code	Book Title	USA / £	Total
	B53	One-Minute Pocket Bible For Teenagers	$ 5 / 3 £	
	B54	One-Minute Daily Devotional (hardback)	$14 / 9 £	
	B55	20 Keys To A Happier Marriage	$ 2 / 1 £	
	B56	How To Turn Mistakes Into Miracles	$ 2 / 1 £	
	B57	31 Secrets Of The Unforgettable Woman	$ 9 / 6 £	
	B58	Mentor's Manna On Attitude	$ 2 / 1 £	
	B59	The Making Of A Champion	$ 6 / 4 £	
	B60	One-Minute Pocket Bible For Men	$ 5 / 3 £	
	B61	One-Minute Pocket Bible For Women	$ 5 / 3 £	
	B62	One-Minute Pocket Bible/Bus. Professionals	$ 5 / 3 £	
	B63	One-Minute Pocket Bible For Truckers	$ 5 / 3 £	
	B64	Mentor's Manna On Achievement	$ 2 / 1 £	
	B65	Mentor's Manna On Adversity	$ 2 / 1 £	
	B66	Greed, Gold And Giving	$ 2 / 1 £	
	B67	Gift Of Wisdom For Champions	$ 8 / 5 £	
	B68	Gift Of Wisdom For Achievers	$ 8 / 5 £	
	B69	Mentor's Manna On The Secret Place	$ 2 / 1 £	
	B70	Gift Of Wisdom For Mothers	$ 8 / 5 £	
	B71	Wisdom - God's Golden Key To Success	$ 7 / 4 £	
	B72	The Double Diamond Daily Devotional	$12 / 8 £	
	B73	Mentor's Manna On Abilities	$ 2 / 1 £	
	B74	The Assignment: Dream/Destiny #1	$10 / 7 £	
	B75	The Assignment: Anointing/Adversity #2	$10 / 7 £	
	B76	The Assignment: Trials/Triumphs #3	$10 / 7 £	
	B77	The Assignment: Pain/Passion #4	$10 / 7 £	
	B78	Wisdom Keys For A Powerful Prayer Life	$ 2 / 1 £	
	B79	7 Obstacles To Abundant Success	$ 2 / 1 £	
	B80	The Greatest Success Habit On Earth	$ 2 / 1 £	
	B81	Born To Taste The Grapes	$ 2 / 1 £	
	B82	31 Reasons People Do Not Receive Their Financial Harvest	$12 / 8 £	
	B83	Gift Of Wisdom For Wives	$ 8 / 5 £	
	B84	Gift Of Wisdom For Husbands	$ 8 / 5 £	
	B85	Gift Of Wisdom For Teenagers	$ 8 / 5 £	
	B86	Gift Of Wisdom For Leaders	$ 8 / 5 £	
	B87	Gift Of Wisdom For Graduates	$ 8 / 5 £	
	B88	Gift Of Wisdom For Brides	$ 8 / 5 £	
	B89	Gift Of Wisdom For Grooms	$ 8 / 5 £	
	B90	Gift Of Wisdom For Ministers	$ 8 / 5 £	
	B91	The Leadership Secrets Of Jesus (hdbk)	$15 /10£	
	B92	Secrets Of The Journey (Vol. 1)	$ 5 / 3 £	
	B93	Secrets Of The Journey (Vol. 2)	$ 5 / 3 £	
	B94	Secrets Of The Journey (Vol. 3)	$ 5 / 3 £	
	B95	Secrets Of The Journey (Vol. 4)	$ 5 / 3 £	

☐ CASH   ☐ CHECK   ☐ MONEY ORDER
☐ CREDIT CARD #   ☐ VISA   ☐ MC   ☐ AMEX

EXPIRATION DATE [ ][ ][ ][ ][ ]   *SORRY NO C.O.D.'s*
Signature _____

TOTAL PAGE 2	$
TOTAL PAGE 1	$
*ADD SHIPPING 10% USA/20% OTHERS	$
CANADA CURRENCY DIFFERENCE ADD 20%	$
TOTAL ENCLOSED	$

PLEASE PRINT

Name

Address

City   State   Zip

Phone ( )   -

32